THE FACE IN THE WATER

1989
Agnes Lynch Starrett
Poetry Prize

The Face in the Water

Nancy Vieira Couto

University of Pittsburgh Press

Published by the University of Pittsburgh Press, Pittsburgh, Pa. 15260
Baker & Taylor International, London
Manufactured in the United States of America

Library of Congress Cataloging-in-Publication Data

Couto, Nancy Vieira, 1942–
   The face in the water / Nancy Vieira Couto.
      p.   cm. — (Pitt poetry series)
   ISBN 0-8229-3652-6. — ISBN 0-8229-5440-0 (pbk.)
   I. Title.   II. Series.
   PS3553.O867F3   1990
   811'.54 — dc20   90-33960
                                                                          CIP

The author and publisher would like to thank the following publications in
which some of these poems first appeared, often in earlier versions: *The
American Poetry Review* ("Elegy"); *Chiaroscuro* ("Lizzie" and "On the Day
of Jayne Mansfield's Death"); *Helicon Nine* ("Finding America" under the
title "Discovering America in the Morning"); *The Iowa Review* ("Living in
the La Brea Tar Pits"); *Poetry Northwest* ("Broiled Haddock," "The Face in
the Water," "I Forget to Eat My Bread," and "Irijay"); *Prairie Schooner*
("1958" and "Wetbacks"); and *Ubu* ("Loosely").

The author wishes to thank the National Endowment for the Arts and the
New York State Creative Artists Public Service Program (CAPS) for fellow-
ships that helped support the writing of these poems. This book might not
have been completed without the tangible encouragement offered by these
fine programs.

*The publication of this book is supported by grants
from the National Endowment for the Arts
in Washington, D.C., a Federal agency,
and the Pennsylvania Council on the Arts.*

for Joe

Contents

PART ONE

Equestrians

Now you are middle-aged you think at least
your face, retrieved from snapshots, enlarged
until the grain is dreamy, gelatinous
as frog's eggs, and your slightly startled smile

disturbs the surface only, will never
glance its accusations off the last
page of a high school yearbook, the page
that everyone remembers, only not

the way it must have been when the train
hurtled out of nowhere like a surprise
quiz on which a final grade depended
that caught them unprepared. You forget

the stories: how they pried one out with knives
and crowbars, how the impact sent the football
hero catapulting from the driver's seat
to land headlong, his beautiful body intact,

the radio miraculously still playing.
That's not what you remember. It's like
coming into the town square at dawn
and finding it deserted and finding them

frozen at seventeen like an Augustus
Saint-Gaudens—that is, frozen and fluid
all at once, unruly hair cowlicked
by wind that tunnels through perpetually open

windows, bronzed arms holding up the roof
of a Chevy that rears and balances, front wheels
spinning at the motes in light that breaks
like water, over and over, and is not broken—

and knowing what's upheld that never breaks
that has no name, only a destination:
Provincetown. And when you turn away
toward offices and storefronts flat as paper

money, you think maybe you owe them
for what you've seen cast in perpetual balance
between the sunstruck bronze and its headlong shadow—
and for the radio, miraculously still playing.

Living in the La Brea Tar Pits

Each morning she is wheeled into the picture
window of her son-in-law's house,
jammed into her selected viewing space
by the table with the lamp and bowling trophy.
The drapes sweep apart like fronds.

She stretches her neck like a brontosaurus
and watches the neighbors, whose names she doesn't
remember. Across the street
two Volkswagens line up like M&M's,
one yellow, one orange.

                              At lunchtime
her daughter broils a small steak, very tender,
saying "Ma, you *must* have meat." But her taste runs
these days to Kellogg's Corn Flakes and baby cereals.
She leans over her plate,
stretching her neck like a brontosaurus,
and mangles a small piece between her tough
gums. The dog waits his turn.

Each evening she is wheeled up close
to the TV in her son-in-law's house.
She watches *Superman* reruns.
In the kitchen, her son-in-law
eats meat and potatoes and talks in a loud voice.
His bowling night—she will have
her daughter to herself. But the TV
picture has gone bad, and the room is dark.
Just last week she could hardly tell if there
were four lovely Lennon sisters, or three.

He returns late—almost eleven—
low scorer on his team. He wants his wife
but there's a dinosaur in his living room, stretching
her neck. It's past her bedtime. He waits his turn.

❀   ❀   ❀

5

Each morning he looks out of the picture
window of his house. Across the street
the neighbors have parked their shiny new Toyotas.
He blinks, as if at something unexpected
and obscene. He moves away,
walking upright, heavy on his bare
heels. He wears pajamas.

                      In the kitchen
he pours orange juice into a paper cup
and takes his medication—two shiny capsules.
His mother-in-law is extinct, and his wife, too.

There is the dog to feed, and he will think of
people to visit. He moves slow, deliberate,
but keeps on moving. The sky is full of birds,
and the Rocky Mountains all have names.

In the evening he turns on the TV
and wedges his fifty-foot frame into his favorite
chair, curling his tail over the armrest.
He watches the third rerun of the Italian
version of *Zorro*. When the horizontal
hold goes haywire, he watches diagonal stripes.

It's not easy to be a tyrannosaurus.
He stands eighteen feet tall, he thuds through life,
what's left. And when he roars, he shows his sharp
stalactites and stalagmites. His grown children
get nervous. He resents them. They wait their turn.

1958

We were not encouraged to become courageous,
and anyway there were those tubes of lipstick
to tempt us with their waxy Crayola shine.
We rehearsed for hours in front of mirrors,

and anyway there were those tubes of lipstick.
We stenciled bows and arrows on our faces.
We rehearsed for hours in front of mirrors,
combing gels and lotions through our hair.

We stenciled bows and arrows on our faces—
all we knew, or needed to, of weapons.
Combing gels and lotions through our hair,
we wound and anchored rollers stuffed with brushes.

All we knew, or needed to, of weapons
were the pegs we used to pin them to our heads.
We wound and anchored rollers stuffed with brushes.
We slept stiffly, dreaming of crowns of thorns.

The pegs we used to pin them to our heads
pinned us, like butterflies displayed on velvet.
We slept stiffly, dreaming of crowns of thorns,
and woke with a soft flutter against the numbness

that pinned us, like butterflies displayed on velvet.
We swaddled our long, tan legs in lacy crinolines
and walked with a soft flutter against the numbness.
We were not, of course, encouraged to be ambitious,

though we swaddled our long, tan legs in lacy crinolines
like the girls who smiled from the pages of *Seventeen*.
We were not, of course, encouraged to be ambitious,
except that each of us hoped to find a boyfriend.

Like the girls who smiled from the pages of *Seventeen*,
we were tempted by that waxy Crayola shine.
Except that each of us hoped to find a boyfriend,
we were not encouraged to become courageous.

Lizzie

A spinster with a mouth like a dam and a heart
like a gyroscope is seen stirring
the shreds of a drab blue dress of Bedford cord
into the kitchen stove. It is Sunday,

three days after the murders. At the trial
witnesses layer their stories like transparencies.
The dress was new, yes, but of a cheap fabric,
badly soiled with paint around the edges,

best got rid of. And so,
because there is no real evidence against her,
nothing (nothing except a spot of blood
on a white petticoat, in back, beneath the placket,

a—how to put it delicately?—souvenir
of her monthly illness), and because
she has been active in church organizations,
and because she is a woman, and a lady,

they acquit her. She stays in that city
where under every jumprope children mock her
to the music of "Ta-ra-ra-boom-de-ay."
She doesn't say, even once, what she is thinking,

but her heart keeps spinning, spinning. If she calls
herself Lizbeth now, it is only
that she always did like Lizbeth better.
She moves to a gabled mansion on a hill

and drives all over the city in a pony
cart. Her investments multiply like fishes.
She entertains some people from the theatre,
an event that shocks her neighbors.

One autumn when the maples turn oppressively
red, she unlocks her smile for the paperboy
who comes in for milk and cookies on his collection
day and is not afraid, or does not know.

She draws a will, leaving money for the care
of animals. And still later,
when her heart, like a child's toy, is winding down
and slowing on its axis,

she is suddenly very surprised to discover
she cannot remember whether it really was paint
or menstrual blood, or blood,
or whether it matters.

Elegy

I

In the beginning, it is all you notice
and everywhere. The houses, white or washed
with color against the sky, climb a trellis
of streets and cross-streets. You repeat the hushed
mantras: Russian, Telegraph, Nob, Potrero,
Sutro. You explore every neighborhood:
North Beach, Chinatown, Embarcadero,
Upper Grant, Marina, Fillmore. You are glad

you came. You catch a cable car up Hyde
to Fisherman's Wharf, where you buy a walk-away
crab cocktail and a loaf of sourdough bread
and sit in the sun. Nearby the drummers ply
their rhythms to the water's. Seagulls call.
The gripman, black and burly, rings his bell.

11

The gripman, black and burly, rings his bell.
You have an Irish coffee at the Buena
Vista and head back over the hill
to your residence club a block away from China-
town. You find a window looking out
across the bay to the lights of Berkeley and Oakland.
That Italian church on Filbert Street is lit
with floods, pulling your focus to the foreground.

You have never before been in a place like this.
The night's last cable car clangs to the barn
and you hold the silence like an empty vase
with a new glaze. You wake to the foghorn
and watch the mops of tule fog that swab
the city. You go downtown. You get a job.

III

In the city you go downtown, you get a job
typing checks in a large insurance office.
You rent a two-room studio on Nob
Hill's slum side, with a wallbed and stained glass
windows that look out on nothing. You dredge
in, make friends, and go out every Friday
night. One Sunday morning you walk to the bridge
and stop, halfway across, to watch the bay,

the sailboats, birds, the islands, the pastel skyline.
A boy on a bike yells "Jump!" You realize
you were thinking of it. About that time the rain
spews sideways up your sleeve, into your eyes.
All winter your umbrella bobs like a buoy.
You were thinking of it, and you don't know why.

IV

You were thinking of it, and you don't know why.
Your neighbors prepare rich food to honor the Year
of the Rooster. In the gym of the Chinese Y,
they arrange the dragon in its glory. Fire-
crackers explode. You go to the parade
and see Grant Avenue swelling like a can
of contaminated soup. You slip the crowd
quietly. About that time the rain

stops. But an astrologer has scheduled
an earthquake for the second week of April,
and people are making jokes. That year they hold
an earthquake party in front of City Hall
at 5:00 A.M., for a community swan song.
The astrologer is, that year, proven wrong.

V

The astrologer is, that year, proven wrong,
but not entirely wrong. The reel of planets
augurs trouble, and the morning papers bring
it in small doses to swallow with coffee and doughnuts
at breaktime. And you know that it was there
all along. And one day you get your turn
when, groping for your keys, you suddenly hear
the other passenger in the empty train-

shaped corridor. Hand zeroes toward your mouth.
You must decide now whether to die
easily or fight. You bare your teeth,
you scream, you wait for what will come—the dry
ice blade, the blaring nozzle. Nothing happens.
He changes his mind. He runs. He has no weapons.

VI

He changes his mind. He runs. He has no weapons.
Pulled once again from the water by the angel
with hairy legs, you live! But your door opens
cautiously, and summer's cold as hell.
You are cold, too, and you mourn the loss
of your own trustfulness. You go to Reno
to learn the art of risk from games of dice
and blackjack. Back in your casino

city at night, you perch on the corner of Jones
and California. Below, a beer glass fills
then drains its neon brew. The dark air preens
like a furred pet electric with stars and jewels.
Three years of rains and dragons circle. And then
one night in the Stockton Tunnel he kills three women.

VII

One night in the Stockton Tunnel he kills three women.
You wear their deaths like pearls of guilt and rage
until the weight snaps the string. At noon
whistle on New Year's Eve, page by page,
you offer another calendar to the barreling
winds. Years later in another place you read
of the mayor and supervisor and the reeling
city that mourns itself more than its dead

servants. But the houses, white or washed
with color against the sky, climb the hills
anyway for others who come flushed
with expectations. Gripmen ring their bells
to night's close punctuation, crystal and amber.
In the end it is what you choose to remember.

I Forget to Eat My Bread

"My heart is smitten, and withered like grass;
so that I forget to eat my bread."—Psalm 102

It was a season kissed with surprises: sap
pulsing up utility poles, pale shoots
sprouting around old porcelain. Night had

no clocks, and cocktail sherry ran like tap
water into jam jars. Parakeets
gashed Australian strobes across the dead

gray walls. The wine meniscus on our cup
rose higher. Waltzabout days we swirled on sheets
of waxed wood. Mirrored, we let the good

times roll, we let the good times roll away.

But the bright green budgie flies into a trap
of meshes. We've misplaced our roller skates,
and sometimes I forget to eat my bread

in the dry season, when the bread is dry.

Wetbacks

Somehow we can't shake the film of water
from our shoulders. This worries
us less than the slow scraping of another day
spent doubled over the hoe between the rows
of lettuce. We go dull as glass-eyed men,
we nod and work on. When seed leaves crumple to specks
and die beneath our thinning strokes, we last.
We have to. And if we dream tonight, we'll dream
that same long field at harvest: tight-wrapped, wrinkled
heads that string out endlessly, like babies.

In another place the women sit between rows
of tables. Working for piece rate at machines
with hypnotic needles, they stitch a steady tattoo
on endless fabric. They don't see
the mold flourishing, fuzzy as velour,
on their damp necks, twining the first white threads
through their neglected hairdos. They keep on feeding
pieces of next season's suburban wardrobe
until their middle fingers curl like fetuses.
They tense when strangers visit.

The grandmothers, knotted in kerchiefs and endless rosaries,
light candles against the hissing fermentation
that steams their wispy napes. They clump and pray
to Our Lady of Guadalupe that the children
will grow clever and strong on frijoles and tortillas
and become doctors or typists or government workers.

So this is why we cross over—to live
the way we live, no better than cucarachas
darting from the drain like thieves in the endless
darkness. We slosh in the unbroken waters
that surround us and our objects and philosophies.
Nothing that we have is clean or dry.

In another place two old uncles are eating tamales
and decorating memories of life before Cesar Chavez.
The one with no teeth smiles. The other tries
to fill two bottomless glasses with cheap wine
from a gallon. They drink to something blurry,
as if through a film of water—something about
a fiesta, something about embroidery,
something about a blind child under a piñata
surrounded by relatives singing and playing accordion.

Night Watch

Someday I will think of this, of walking
across the Keizersgracht at night under a silence
high, tight, and clear

as a bell jar, a silence that protects
not from sound, not from the lapping of water
against walls or the sudden chirps and da-rrrings

of balloon-tired bicycles with saddlebags,
but from language as I know it, all its phonemes
of imposition. I will have to force myself

out of myself, wear my luck like glaze,
to accept the unarticulated warnings
of light-strung waterways, remembering

stars that connect their own dots
restring themselves into new configurations.
So the bear's long tail or the handle

of a spoon becomes a bright, arched doorway
into the Leidsegracht, into the rest of the journey.

*　　*　　*

A tram parts the crowd on the Leidsestraat
and the crowd accepts it. No one is hurt.

All the cafés on the Leidseplein
are full of me. My lanterns of beer
could be rescue. Or warning. When I travel

I keep my mouth shut, walk the bricked
sidewalks as if I know each brick.
It is easy to be a foreigner when the city is dark

as a Rembrandt, to slip into canal houses
and out again without touching doorknobs
or windowsashes. It is easy to be water

and to make wider circles, call myself Singel,
Herengracht, Keizersgracht, Prinsengracht.
This is what I want my death to be like.

You Bet Your Life

In the beginning, the word
is shown to the audience.
And although it's a common
word, something I see
every day, I don't say it.

We talk about my life,
but he won't take it seriously.

And after I've wagered
all my money, and lost it,
and after I didn't know
who was buried in Grant's tomb
and I've said my good-byes
to Groucho and George
and I'm walking toward the wings
feeling like a failure,

I guess I must say something right
under my breath,
because the ceiling divides
and the duck
comes down and gives me a hundred dollars.

Tea Party

"Vassar girls attend teas;
Bridgewater girls give them."
—The Dean of Women

So there you are, in wispy veil and hat,
out to out-Vassar Vassar, macaroons
crumbling from the saucer that you balance
with kid gloves. Dizzy from the bargains
you thought you'd struck, you've swapped your last ounce
of naiveté for that
die-cast innocence the Quaker whalemen
fingered as they steered their weighty payload
toward Boston, their wake a bright divide
unyielding as the double line drawn down
a ledger. *We mind our business, we pray for peace.*
You wobble across the room on high heels,
a ropewalker. The waves are sloped as china
teacups and the ocean churns with whales,
schools of them. With studied legerdemain the
expression on your face
says sugar-and-milk-please when the faux
Indians moccasin up the gangplank
looking *so* familiar. And only when they've sunk
your whole consignment of exotic thus
taxable teas do you lean back, close your eyes,
and let the bloodyolked sun draw delicate ratlines
on your veiled face. They stood for peace, those captains,
and you the initiate stand for your school and your class.

PART TWO

Promises

Get it in writing: that's the first principle
of business, Gaspar knew. And the king agreed
the second was the balance sheet, debits
sashaying in the harbor. Those caravels,
for instance, ambivalent as virgins
worrying arrangements of cross-stitch rosebuds
over dishtowels and bedlinens, blushing
in the wash of the setting sun. It was Gaspar's
money there: the polished hulls, the dowries
of shrouds and sails. Then there was the matter
of the biscuits, hard as coins, from the royal
ovens. Who counted them, recorded them,
carried them to the docks under the fringed
night that covered Europe like a widow's
kerchief? The king knew it was good agribusiness
to press wheat into rations for the voyage
that started out like all good business ventures:
on paper. Accruing to the west,
across the ocean's spread, were the inventories:
trees of such a perfect height and thickness
they could be hybrids bred for a second life
on shipboard, taproot anchored in the keel,
skeleton branches. And the well-formed natives'
good looks and raw dignity: such a labor force
to set before the king. As for the Northwest
Passage, well, maybe next time, after spring
loosened winter's icy-fingered grip
on inland waters. Trees and slaves were good
as gold, anyhow. Gaspar had it made.

So why was he so strange? When they loaded
one of the ships with samples of the booty
and a few choice Indians, those who'd always wanted
to visit Europe, why did Gaspar say:

Go without me. Tell the king it's bigger
than either of us dreamed of. Tell him thank you
for promising more than he could deliver.
Me? I think I'll just explore
the coastline where it loops and doubles over
and dots itself like some gigantic signature
I can't decipher. Go. Don't worry about me.

The Indians were a hit. All that season
fashionable senhoras embroidered feathers
on petticoats and camisoles, while husbands
moved their lips, struggling to interpret
the moon-sealed contract scrolling on the western
horizon, as if envious of an absence
rife with promises.

Irijay

To see the irijay is to receive
easy on the tongue some tenuous disk,
some token that, even as it dissolves,
contains. To see the irijay
is to give back or up whatever luck
exacts for gnosis: nescience, maybe. So

myths are made. This is one rara avis
you won't see on *Wild Kingdom.* Although sometimes

freaks turn up that from excess or lack
vibrate off the ground: cameos
or tokens. Such, the albino buffalo
on *Rin Tin Tin,* the one that Rusty saw,
the one that saved him. All of us need saving

and we save: buffalo nickels, bus
tokens, our mothers' cameos,
intaglios—whatever's in relief
against quotidian tempera. And myth
sops our habit. So the irijay
has become bigger than a bird: its grace,
unrevealed, more glorious than the rending
of the mist by cardinal or tanager.

Does that make sense? The Indians had a word,
opossum: it meant "white beast." The week
my mother died I saw one on the street,
misplaced and scared, staring down my headlamps
like the Nowhere Man. I knew what it meant,

I'm a receiver. But the irijay
signifies by omission, defined
only by peripheries of desire
that silhouette its absence. And so
nobody sees it. There is no irijay.

The rest is dream.

29

II

We'd had, that day, a long
talk about the nature of our relationship.
Trés civilized. And, as we slept, outflung
arms and legs and dreams must have described
stark bilateral symmetry: snuggled ass
to ass, we canted outward like wings
extended for flight, all our tokens
powerless to save us, and our separate lives
cameo parts in a movie.

The cry
was something like a trumpet's, but flared
out onto the visual: familiar,
elusive: a flapping shape I'd shadowed
down assorted aisles to lose each time
I almost touched. And there I'd be, instead,
running my fingers over plastic beads
of a rosary, or clasping a plastic candle,
or screwing together the two plastic halves
of an applicator. And nothing apprehended.
The cry, which could no more be apprehended
than the promise of ceremony—everyone knows
the wedding album's just a mock-up, stills
from an old movie starring Nelson Eddy
and Jeanette MacDonald—was echoed
by a second cry (this is a dream, remember)
that skewered all my senses. I was, in sleep,
pure audience.

There were, then, two of them
zeroing toward each other, wafer wings
stiff as gliders' wings. And though they were
identical in size, shape, and fury,
their snowcrust feathers kissed with shimmers of rainbow,

I knew with basal horror they were female
and male, come in battle, and because
they equaled each other, neither could lose without winning,
neither could win without losing.
So feathers flew, and through the squall I watched
wing beat on bloody wing, beak
stab and parry.

                    Here the plot drifts
and three potential denouements, in turn,
are inverted and obscured, as if by snow:

(1) With simultaneous, precise strokes
each kills the other. (2) As above,
except that, after an interval, they stir
and fumble into flight together as if
slightly tossed askew and needing to compensate.
(3) As above, but from the rubble
a single bird rebuilds itself intact
to blaze a perfect path across the sky.

III

It's an encroachment, really, these creatures,
the way they pop up when we most expect them
to absorb culpability or credit
for our own saving gestures. They're freaks,
all of them. To see the irijay
is to want too much, to wipe that want with myth
and polish till it vibrates with our own
aching likenesses, to give and take
off the same paten. We're the real freaks,
askew between quotidian tempera
and spectra, carved in some sort of relief
and fumbling to save ourselves.

On the Day of Jayne Mansfield's Death

he offers me a ride to the laundromat
in his white '59 Ford. We stop at Oscar's
to buy detergent. They bunch around the radio—
old Oscar, two women in housedresses
and anklesocks, and a cat that flicks its tail
to the static. Of course it's inconceivable
that it should happen, that we should hear the news
here in the Adirondacks, where nothing happens.

There is nobody else in the laundromat.
We stuff machines, measure out the Tide,
plunge quarters into boxes. He unrolls
his sleeves, removes his shirt and throws it in,
watches it disappear. We sit by the window
and talk about the trip he's just returned from.
Salinas, the labor camp. The whores
in Salt Lake City. Selling a pool cue
for gas money somewhere in Missouri.
I listen, hungry. I know he's only nineteen.
He's wearing the cleanest undershirt that I've ever seen.

Suddenly I'm spinning in a machine,
pelted with the centrifugal slap of mink,
sable, satin. Bras the size of spinnakers
tack across the far side of the Maytag.
My hair spools out with the blonde bounce of silk.
His muscles are bigger and shinier than Mickey Hargitay's.

Finding America

I. *She Pits Her Silhouette*

So Palos recedes, a shrinking circle
nested inside circles: España,
Europa, Orbis stretched flat as linen
bleaching in the sun. That was the old
theology. The woman, now an admiral
and a player, paces the sterncastle
of the flagship *Santa Maria,* rehearsing stories
told in Portugal: how pine boughs drifted
up beaches at Fayal and Graçiosa,
how one day two corpses that bore no feature
of any Christian people washed like pine boughs
over the rocks of Flores. She is thirty-
three, and her hair is white. She pits
her silhouette against the ocean's, wagering
everything on its symmetry. Everything.

I never imagined that my life
could be a mariner's run down the latitude
to Cipangu and nightingales. If I keep
two reckonings, it's not to deceive the sailors,
who don't trust me anyhow, but to mark
my own nightly undoing of the distance.
Because at night I see myself in Genoa
with the old dream, the limp and familiar doll.
I see myself carding wool, combing the matted
fleece across bent nails. Looking for babies
in the haphazard patterns of seeds in halved
fruit. Feeling the breath of tall foreigners
hot on the honeyed breeze that perplexes
me as I bend in moonlight over my washbasin.

She keeps the log in a schoolgirl hand, unspooling
threads of symbols, auguries. A marvelous

branch of fire that topples through the waves
not five leagues from her prow. Grass that grows
on the ocean. She leans out like a figurehead,
sights along her palm. We are almost
there, she tells them, there, don't be afraid.

I am afraid, I am afraid, I am afraid.

II. *She Sweetens the Pot*

When wind stops, the ocean silvers: a looking
glass. Their trust is cracking. Three ships
are so far out of the world, the world has no
rules. Though she talks faith, talk is air,
spiritus nonsanctus. Her heart is hollow,
too. All her lust is for land: dirt
more than her portion of gold, more than salvation.

September 25th: The captain of the *Pinta*
sights Cathay—those tantalizing amber
waves of Asian grain. *Gloria in excelsis:*
three crews as one pulse, as one mission.
The admiral kneels to thank the Virgin,
but dawn reveals just a tufted cloudbank
teasing the horizon. *Kyrie eleison.*

Christe eleison. The grumbling increases.
Iberian faces are cisterns of plot: Basta!
This foreigner's crazy, a witch
of ambition. Catching their looks, their uneasy
gestures, she sweetens the pot: *Sailors, whoever
first outlines Eastern delights over western curvature,
to him I'll award silk hose and a velvet doublet.*

October 12th: A crewman calls out
in the dark, entreating "Orient" to that raw
landfall, that low breast of promise, nipple
of hope (not illusion) two leagues to the west:
San Salvador. Wisely, they drop anchor
to wait for morning. He claims his prize,
lowering his eyes. *Roderigo! Not the ones I'm wearing!*

III. *She Accepts Their Gifts*

> A white woman comes from the eastern
>   sky on a big white bird.
> Her hair is spun from the cloud that holds
>   no rain. Her robe is red
> as the western sky. She is the Mother
>   of Wind and Water.

The island is small and low. Bronze-colored
people watch me read my proclamation.
They appear docile. Their hair is straight. They must
be Indians. All of them are naked,
but I pretend not to be embarrassed.

Land. It slaps against my rolling balance.
My stomach pitches. They bring me ornaments
hammered of gold in trade for hawks'
bells, glass beads, red caps.
I shall be a rich woman soon.

> The sun smiles on the white woman's
>   footsteps. We hear her words
> but not her secrets. We offer cotton, gold
>   baubles, and bright birds.
> She accepts our gifts. She is the Mother
>   of Wind and Water.

IV. *She Shares Miscalculations*

Thus the Indian Ocean beyond the Ganges
explodes with cays, and the same story always:
Go to the next island. The gold you seek
to deliver from us is tucked like a seventh-moon child
in a woman. So three ships tack and jog,
genuflecting at each station like three nuns,
wind bloating the bellies of their white
habits, till they hear of Colba.

                    Colba?
That island is no woman but a universe
bold with seed, projectile in luxuriance.
Even the sea is polite there, the waves
doffing spumed caps to the apparition
of an unknown king appareled in wild purslane
and amaranth.

                I thought it was Cathay
at first. So large. And no perceptible
end to our astonishments. Cotton
basking in the dream of perpetual harvest:
flowers and bolls, some opened, others about to
burst, all on one tree, like a family.
Carrotlike roots swelling with deformities: mealy
to the tongue and sweet as chestnuts. In a native
fisherman's hut we puzzled at a dog
that had no bark, as if it knew no danger.
The land is high as Sicily, felicitous
for the pleasures and chinoiseries of the Grand
Khan.

        But it was not Cathay. The Indians
told by signs of a wide girdle of water,

37

a twenty days' journey by canoe. I knew
then that I had found Japan, Cipangu.

Imagine cutting through the membranous
skin of the world, stripping it with one careful
flick, pressing it flat, letting it tear
and spread at the poles like fruit peel. Imagine
razoring down those longitudes that parenthesize
America, pulling that segment from its backing
and concealing it. Now imagine gluing together
whatever's left and simmering it in boiled
sugar until translucent as the lighted
globes displayed in stationers' windows. Only
this globe is shaped like a lemon or a citron.
She does the best she can.

      The land is sweet
in natural wealth, although these Japanese
are not what I expected and I find
no gold. Where is the emperor's mighty palace
that Marco Polo wrote of, roofed with gold
instead of lead? The chambers lined with puffed
tiles, each a pure biscuit of gold?
Where are the golden bowls? The golden eggs?
I thought to see parades of merchants swathed
in gold lamé. But they go naked, nor
does gold leaf sprout from enameled trees.
Every bush, branch, tendril screams with green.
I should have shipped a botanist, not a Hebrew
interpreter, to tell which of these herbs
are marketable as medicines in Spain.
The Japanese prize a variety of dried
leaf of unknown purpose. Dyes and spices
need to be gathered, labeled, exported.
That there are mussels suggests there may be pearls,
but I find no gold.

Nor any emperor, either,
barefoot along the lapped, white shoreline, tracing
the fringes of his realm. So she instructs
two Spaniards and two Indians: *Find him.*
Take these Latin passports and some strings
of beads to buy food with. Follow
that rise to the crevice of his corporeal
worth, his vein of gold, inscrutable heart.
Don't say that your admiral is a woman.

In her dream the emperor's composite
visage, like a police illustrator's
patchwork, vibrates. The *Santa Maria,* anchored
in the soporific wash of Puerto Gibara,
vibrates from the jackhammer of her question:
How will she subjugate him, and will
she want to?

They return six days later
with stories of a village of palm-branch houses
pitched as in a camp. Hanging furniture
called *hamaca,* made of cotton string.
The mysterious leaf explained: Roll it tight,
hold one tip to a firebrand and the other
to a nostril, and inhale. Olé.
But no emperor's cache of gold. She entertains
the local *cacique* over wine, salt meat,
and garlic.

Of course I'm disappointed,
not surprised. Two nights before full moon
I measured altitude of the North Star
with a quadrant. Though nightingales sing arias,
this land is not Cipangu but a piece
of mainland Asia—not Cathay but near
Cathay—an uninitiated kingdom.

She slips the *Santa Maria* and camps
on a cushion of grass under slit
palms and a gibbous moon like God's eye.

I dreamed I felt the earth push so hard
it woke me. Startled from sleep I pushed to touch
back. But my touch, fluid, took
Colba's outline, melting to a thin-
spent glaze over vegetation, an eighth
layer of skin. Neural, nameless, pure
receptor, I suddenly knew this land I lay on:
Cuba. We twirled in a watery lasso.

Golden island: Pulling toward wakefulness
I hold these intimations of your future spasms,
given me even as I shared miscalculations
that made a sailor of a weaver's daughter
and blew her to this grassy bed, the taste
of roast dog still perplexing her palate:
your cigars, sugar, the yellow fever,
revolution and a leader named Fidel.
Your children will load rifles in gymnasiums,
slamming magazines. This has nothing
to do with me, middle-aged offspring of another
hemisphere, who measured the wrong star
and found a world. No one shall ever know

that there's a clearing between coming foreign
to each other and becoming foreign
to each other. Island: I'll send horses.

Ice Museum

In the first room there's a diorama
of the Glacial Epoch in New England.
I know this ice as well as I know stone
walls that crisscross pastures in my town
to mark them off into rectangular plots
like pillows, embroidered *yours* and *mine*.

The next room is the sculpture gallery.
We trace separate circles, clockwise and counter,
before the frozen beauty of the stilled
Terpsichores, Calliopes. We meet
in silence at the pedestal of the mechanized
Isis, poised, cyclical and iciclical.
I know this ice as well as I know my own
body's hollow stem. Inside my down
jacket, I'm glazed with sweat, clammy.
Goddess of the wine glass, she slowly
fills and, like a wine glass, too swiftly
empties. She is the ultimate pellucid
woman, except for that nacreous heart
clenching and releasing like a fist.

You have already entered the third room,
the one that holds the intricately chiseled
farmhouse. Cross-sectioned, cryogenic,
it's the honeycomb, scraped. The popsicle
halves of childhood stacked like Lincoln Logs
with all the syrup sucked away. I seek you
like a child covetous of another's toys, aching
to rearrange the inch-high snowperson family
from room to crystalline room. Why do you stop me
cold with anthracite eyes? Don't you know
they wobble but they won't fall down? You think

you know your ice as well as I know mine.
Your scarf flutters between us. Your breath is frosty.

In the last room is the exhibit entitled "Practical
Applications." A display case contains ice cube
trays, assorted: Rubbermaid, metal, novelty,
pornographic. There are cocktails in the lobby
on our way out. I balance mine in a mittened
palm and watch the blocks clink together,
bounce apart. Acknowledge: My other hand,
hidden still deep in its handwarmer pocket,
is ice, I know, as well as I know bone
is ice, digit is ice. Sugared.
Sharp. Savage. Scared. I wish I could touch you.

Broiled Haddock

"And they gave him a piece of a broiled fish. . . .
And he took it, and did eat before them."—St. Luke

Believing's more than seeing. You bear witness
your way—I, mine. Just last night
didn't you touch your finger to my wound,
press the lingering flesh until it gave

and parted? Wasn't that a miracle?
So I, asking less, scour the ordinary
fluorescence of supermarkets for evidence
to drench with clarified butter, dredge with crumbs.

Sometimes I make the sign of the cross in parsley.
You're coming for dinner. Doesn't my kitchen table
shine like an altar? Linen, lace, and candlesticks.
Bread on a salver. White wine. Artichokes.

Broiled haddock. These are my offerings.
Take, eat: That will be your testimony.

You Have Shown Me a Strange Image,
and We Are Strange Prisoners

You grow impatient while I focus, fiddle
with the aperture, forget to cock the shutter.

reflex   Your mouth droops, sets in what I call your pissed-
off look, the look you wear in all your formal
photographs. And if I try to snare you
with wide-angle lens, autofocus, Tri-X,
and flash, all I get is blank surprise
before the mirror flips. The mirror plays
the same old game, I play the same old tricks
badly. Frame after frame you slip through
my viewfinder, leaving not-quite-normal
thumbprints and toothmarks, a pressed
smile under glass, montage built of silver
reckless light. The mirror's in the middle.

               ❖   ❖   ❖

I shouldn't need to put my faith in magic.
After all, it's only Dektol. I control

chemistry what it does, and why. The paper curls
perceptibly, as if startled in the act
of becoming an egg, a fertile egg with a thin
opalescent shell still unhardened
by the real world. I must not love you enough

or I wouldn't need to put my faith in magic.
Checking the clock, I slide the paper in
with one hand, with the other start a careful
rocking so you'd think I held an ocean
in a tray. In seconds you are born
again against my doubt under the safe
light in a dark room. The fetal curves

of cheek and brow, your embryonic smile
define themselves, darken, assert the shapes
I've captured. Then the hypo eases out
the undertow, teeming with grains of silver
possibilities. Out of the wash you look
remarkably like a photo of yourself,
but not yourself. I must not love you enough.

❋   ❋   ❋

The image doesn't hold without belief.
For all the gentle miracles of silver
safelight we see each other dimly under safe

light in a dark room. Although it's half
hide-and-seek, a trick with lens and mirror,
the image doesn't hold without belief.

And even if I did love you enough
to print full frame for each stroke of the shutter,
we'd see each other dimly under safe

light, for what is love if not a rough
projection from the negative? On paper
the image doesn't hold without belief

in burning, dodging love, and the proof
fades fast. How can we hope for better
than to see each other dimly under safe

light in the dark, cropped in the dark, deaf
to hints of coded detail even pure
image couldn't hold without belief?
We see each other dimly under safe light.

45

Loosely

"They touched both my eyes
And I touched the dew on their hem."
—Leonard Cohen

The bed accepts us, rustling like a glazed
sheet of butcher's paper. A mélange
of language and moist parts, we wrap ourselves up
the only way we know: loosely. It's hard

to nourish in a world where all the world
starves. So I explore the creased sack
that hoods your other eyes, try to feed
sight, fingertips cool and quick as spoons.

Not enough. Nor is it when you probe
the hungers strung like beads along my fringed
hem. A mélange of fingers and tongues,
we make each other whole as best we can

while the world starves. This parable: Though parched
we nurse, relentless, on rivers of living water.

The Face in the Water

I

That was a time for panic: our bodies
unfolding, those new, disturbing billows
of roses. At school we shuffled circles,
tethered to gossip. Tracing circles
on calendars, we counted out our bodies'
rosaries, floating dreams on billows

of boys' faces. Why, then, did our teachers
pick that year to send us out for softball
every recess, unless they felt uneasy
at our contagious blossoming? Uneasy
with dodgeball and jumprope, with our teachers,
and with the boys we dreamed of, we played softball

at recess. Laced into saddleshoes, petticoats,
and fielder's mitts, we must have made a fluffy
harlequinade of missed connections, striking
through pollen-charged air, mostly striking
out. At the plate our starched petticoats
hung stiff as clocks (but in the outfield, fluffy

butterflies). Always, from the woods,
the low, digestive gurgle of running
water. One day one of us hit a home
run—rookie's luck. As she circled home,
one of us scrabbled bravely into the woods
to find the ball and came out, flushed, running

like mad, shouting something about a rising
face in the creek, a dead man's arm shooting up
like a tree, the ball lost forever. *We should tell
the police. At least the teachers. Wait! Don't tell
anyone. Bullet holes? One eye open? Rising
like bread dough.* One of us threw up.

*And the hand? Wearing a high school ring?
Don't go in there!* None of us did. And we said

47

nothing, needing that Pushmi-Pullyu fear
to fix our panic on. It was the fear
that saved us, though the story didn't ring
true, not really. And none of us ever said

much about it afterwards. We introduced
overhand throwing, real rules, and we got better
at softball, kicking up crinoline and racing
fear around the bases. We were racing
time, too. Our mothers introduced
us to what they called the facts of life (better

to tell it their way lest we learn the truth,
perhaps). They sat us down in perfumed bedrooms,
read shyly from that illustrated booklet
they'd all sent away for. *Don't ever let
a boy touch you.* If they had known the truth,
that when we closed our eyes in our pink bedrooms

we saw that face bobbing and ballooning
like an ideogram for fear, they would never
have bothered with those diagrams, drawn badly,
all pellets, traps, and tubes, like some badly
conceived pinball machine, some ballooning
gadget out to get us that we'd never

conquer. Pulled toward that field
of nameless force, we conquered fear by fearing
and stuck with softball. That spring we all looked
differently at the world we'd overlooked.
The boys would sometimes stop and help us field
practice balls. We got deft and wild at fearing.

48

II

This is a time for panic: our bodies
tremulous as mimosa, set to fold
at a finger's touch. This is no time to waste
time, and so, having no time to waste,
I have taken a lover. I listen to my body's
rhythms, lying sleepless in the fold

of his sleeping body, and I see in the dark
that softball game unfolding in reflected
light: the ring of bases in a field
of obstacles. Then, it was the field
I ached to comprehend, the guarded dark
side of the game. Now it's the light, reflected

off canvas and rubber markers: the geometry
of safety, which has little to do with fear,
less to do with running against the clock,
touching bases. After all this time and clock-
work, I've learned some plain geometry,
simple mineralogy, and the fear

has crystallized: I know what I'm afraid
of. Tonight, as headlamps crest and break
through Venetian blinds, my lover's face
surfaces, then sinks. It is a face
under water. Shimmying. Broken. I'm afraid
to look. Afraid refraction, that break

between love and structure, will finally prove
unbridgeable. Afraid I'll see the bobbing
face of a drifting stranger caught by incident
light, treading light. This incident
plays itself inside out, as if to prove
some theorem: Sometimes my own bobbing

image ripples back from underwater
surfaces. Adolescent and elusive,

49

I lift the bat, balance its heft. The pressure
of the water is intense, and to add to the pressure
the bases are loaded. Through the water
I see them, phosphorescent and elusive

and schematic, though I can't make out the faces
looping over them like heavenly bodies
in orbit. Down here it's all slow motion
and soft: we swing, we drift and bob, we motion
to no one and everyone, blurring faces
in the water. We are in over our bodies.

Magalhães' Last Testament

Having always been a person of more stamina
than energy, I'm not surprised to find myself
in the Philippines, although these wide-eyed natives
are surprised. By their faces you'd think
I was a ghost of some sort, or the evil eye.
Make a *figo*, I tell them, make a *figo*
and I'll go away, I promise. But no,
something terrible must have happened, and I'm to blame.
Their arrows are sharp and my language
splatters like birdshit. I guess stamina
won't pull me through this time. Still, I'm not sorry
I work for whoever pays, don't ask about life insurance,
and never keep promises. The strait
was something else though, a line payed out in coils
before me. I take no credit for that.
It must have been maneuvering that twisted,
rock-walled maze that did it—the smell
of something in the williwaws, something final
blasting down the fjords toward the ocean.
Nothing was familiar—not breathing,
not seeing, not thinking. The crazy thing
was even on short rations I felt full,
ready to burst, like a big glutton.
I said to myself, Fernão, this is too much,
and knew it was over. If I had known the Pacific
goes on forever—but by then I was a machine,
all gears and pulleys, winding my own self up.
Better that way. I think if I've learned
anything from this, it's that a man
can go halfway around the world, no further,
or, in plainer words, can go in one
direction only: away. Oh, natives,
listen to my words while they are liquid
testament to a workaday kind of travel:
I never meant to sail so goddam far.
I was just doing my job.

51

About the Author

Nancy Vieira Couto was born in New Bedford, Massachusetts, in 1942. She studied at Bridgewater State College and at Cornell University, where she received her M.F.A. in 1980. Her poems have appeared in *The American Poetry Review, The Iowa Review, Prairie Schooner, Poetry Northwest,* and other literary magazines. In 1987 she received a National Endowment for the Arts Poetry Fellowship. *The Face in the Water* was selected from seven hundred manuscripts submitted to the 1989 Agnes Lynch Starrett Poetry Prize. Maxine Kumin served as the final judge. Couto, who lives in Ithaca, New York, is on the staff of Cornell University Press.

PITT POETRY SERIES
Ed Ochester, General Editor

Dannie Abse, *Collected Poems*
Claribel Alegría, *Flowers from the Volcano*
Claribel Alegría, *Woman of the River*
Maggie Anderson, *Cold Comfort*
Robin Becker, *Giacometti's Dog*
Michael Benedikt, *The Badminton at Great Barrington; Or, Gustave Mahler & the Chattanooga Choo-Choo*
Michael Burkard, *Ruby for Grief*
Siv Cedering, *Letters from the Floating World*
Lorna Dee Cervantes, *Emplumada*
Robert Coles, *A Festering Sweetness: Poems of American People*
Nancy Vieira Couto, *The Face in the Water*
Kate Daniels, *The Niobe Poems*
Kate Daniels, *The White Wave*
Toi Derricotte, *Captivity*
Norman Dubie, *Alehouse Sonnets*
Stuart Dybek, *Brass Knuckles*
Odysseus Elytis, *The Axion Esti*
Jane Flanders, *Timepiece*
Gary Gildner, *Blue Like the Heavens: New & Selected Poems*
Bruce Guernsey, *January Thaw*
Barbara Helfgott Hyett, *In Evidence: Poems of the Liberation of Nazi Concentration Camps*
Milne Holton and Paul Vangelisti, eds., *The New Polish Poetry: A Bilingual Collection*
David Huddle, *Paper Boy*
Phyllis Janowitz, *Temporary Dwellings*
Lawrence Joseph, *Curriculum Vitae*
Lawrence Joseph, *Shouting at No One*
Etheridge Knight, *The Essential Etheridge Knight*
Bill Knott, *Poems: 1963–1988*
Ted Kooser, *One World at a Time*
Ted Kooser, *Sure Signs: New and Selected Poems*
Larry Levis, *Winter Stars*
Larry Levis, *Wrecking Crew*
Robert Louthan, *Living in Code*
Tom Lowenstein, tr., *Eskimo Poems from Canada and Greenland*
Irene McKinney, *Six O'Clock Mine Report*
Archibald MacLeish, *The Great American Fourth of July Parade*

Peter Meinke, *Night Watch on the Chesapeake*
Peter Meinke, *Trying to Surprise God*
Judith Minty, *In the Presence of Mothers*
Carol Muske, *Applause*
Carol Muske, *Wyndmere*
Leonard Nathan, *Carrying On: New & Selected Poems*
Leonard Nathan, *Holding Patterns*
Kathleen Norris, *The Middle of the World*
Sharon Olds, *Satan Says*
Alicia Suskin Ostriker, *Green Age*
Alicia Suskin Ostriker, *The Imaginary Lover*
Greg Pape, *Black Branches*
James Reiss, *Express*
David Rivard, *Torque*
William Pitt Root, *Faultdancing*
Liz Rosenberg, *The Fire Music*
Maxine Scates, *Toluca Street*
Richard Shelton, *Selected Poems, 1969-1981*
Peggy Shumaker, *The Circle of Totems*
Arthur Smith, *Elegy on Independence Day*
Gary Soto, *Black Hair*
Gary Soto, *The Elements of San Joaquin*
Gary Soto, *The Tale of Sunlight*
Gary Soto, *Where Sparrows Work Hard*
Tomas Tranströmer, *Windows & Stones: Selected Poems*
Chase Twichell, *Northern Spy*
Chase Twichell, *The Odds*
Leslie Ullman, *Dreams by No One's Daughter*
Constance Urdang, *Alternative Lives*
Constance Urdang, *Only the World*
Ronald Wallace, *People and Dog in the Sun*
Ronald Wallace, *Tunes for Bears to Dance To*
Belle Waring, *Refuge*
Cary Waterman, *The Salamander Migration and Other Poems*
Bruce Weigl, *A Romance*
Robley Wilson, *Kingdoms of the Ordinary*
Robley Wilson, *A Pleasure Tree*
David Wojahn, *Glassworks*
David Wojahn, *Mystery Train*
Paul Zimmer, *Family Reunion: Selected and New Poems*